THE REBEL
NEGOTIATOR'S
GUIDE
—— TO ——
BUYING
—— A ——
CAR

ISBN: 978-0692911396

Formatting by Mallory Rock and The Illustrated Author

TABLE OF CONTENTS

FOREWORD

I have always been amazed at how much the average person fears negotiation. Many see it as a battle full of screaming, yelling, and fist-pounding, where neither party walks away happy. I, however, look at negotiation as a puzzle and an opportunity to influence people to reach an agreement.

I teach negotiation workshops all over the world. As a member of the Negotiations Center of Excellence for one of the largest IT and consulting services providers, I teach these workshops to help participants understand their strengths and weaknesses as negotiators, enhance their negotiation acumen, remain self-aware at the negotiating table, and fine-tune their use of negotiation methodology that can be utilized in a principled and disciplined way.

I strictly adhere to the "4x7" approach—four principles and seven elements—that affects the success of every negotiation, personal and professional. On Day 1 of the workshop, I introduce this approach in the context of a buyer walking into a dealership to negotiate buying a new car. I begin there because we've all experienced negotiating to buy a car, but it still causes plenty of anxiety and stress, even for experienced negotiators.

Since anxiety and stress seem to be givens in buying a car, I have devoted this book to prepare you for negotiating your new car purchase so the experience will be less traumatic and, perhaps, even pleasant. My approach for negotiating to buy a new car (and to trade in your vehicle, if applicable) is built on the same negotiation methodology that is the foundation for the $5 billion in technology and outsourcing agreements that I have successfully negotiated during my career.

As you read this book, you can take comfort in the fact that I have cut my teeth and inflicted plenty of wounds (in the interest of full disclosure, I have received a few as well) at the negotiating table over the past twenty years with some of the most difficult and aggressive negotiators on the planet—Fortune 500 buyers and their procurement organizations, elite law firms, and third-party advisory firms. Many of those experiences were extremely frustrating as they included inexperienced negotiators and inferior negotiation processes. That frustration inspired me to lead a rebellion focused on achieving effective and efficient negotiations and made me proud to earn the title, "The Rebel Negotiator."

After you read this book and are seated at the car dealership, I strongly encourage you to focus on the 4x7 approach methodology, remain disciplined, and channel your inner Rebel Negotiator. Ultimately, that should allow you to inhale that sweet new-car smell knowing that you negotiated a great deal.

INTRODUCTION

IT'S TIME TO FACE REALITY

It is highly likely that at some point in your adult life you may have said these words:

1. It's too old.

2. It lacks style.

3. It's not safe.

4. The mileage is too high.

5. The technology is outdated.

6. The repair and maintenance bills are exorbitant.

7. The warranty is about to expire.

8. I need more horsepower and torque.

9. The paint is dull and the car has too many scratches and dents.

10. The incentives and financing options are too good to pass up.

11. Everyone has a new car but me.

No matter which statement you made, you probably decided this: It's time to buy a new car. You probably made that decision with a high level of excitement, as the possibilities seemed endless—sedan, coupe, convertible, pickup truck, minivan, manufacturer, power plant, transmission, color, wheels, interior, and plenty of other options. Nothing feels better than driving that new car home. And that new-car smell ... what can I say? It is heavenly.

Once the excitement wears off, however, feelings of stress and anxiety usually surface. Then your comments might be like these:

1. I hate going to the dealership to buy a new car.

2. The process is too complicated—there are simply too many options.

3. I want to avoid the entire negotiation process.

4. I am afraid to negotiate.

5. I am not a good negotiator.

6. I feel trapped once I walk into the car dealership.

7. I don't like car salespeople.

8. I never feel like I am getting a good deal.

9. I don't feel like the dealership is being honest with me.

10. Can I call someone to negotiate the purchase on my behalf?

11. Is there an online buying service I can use so I just have to show up and sign the paperwork?

The desire to avoid negotiation or the general fear of it is typical. In the negotiation workshops I facilitate, I try to understand the level of comfort people have with negotiation, in general, and, specifically, with negotiating the purchase of a new car.

Workshop participants' feedback about their level of comfort with negotiation consistently focused on these four key areas: (1) a general aversion to conflict, and negotiation for many people is the epitome of conflict; (2) a fear of losing or a fear of hurting the relationship with the other party; (3) a fear of being in an ambiguous situation where the outcome is unclear; and (4) an inability or reluctance to ask for things, which results in lost opportunities for negotiation.

If we think about those four areas in the context of buying a new car, the level of discomfort grows exponentially. Going to the car dealership to negotiate the purchase of a new car and the value of a trade-in for your car can yield plenty of conflict on both sides of the negotiating table. Tempers may flare, fists may be pounded, and leaving the table altogether is common. As for the fear of losing, people want to feel like they got a "good deal," and that is not always true once the car is safely in the buyer's garage and the dust has settled. Although maintaining a strong relationship with your car salesperson is not that important, there are few other transactions where the outcome is so ambiguous given the variability in price and other terms. Finally, many new-car buyers are reluctant to consider their full range of options, underestimate their negotiating strength, and miss opportunities to capture that elusive "good deal."

Let's be clear: The Internet has drastically changed the car-buying experience. Potential buyers have tremendous amounts of data at their fingertips via their smartphone or tablet, and many are using this information to their advantage in negotiations. A 2014 study by market research company JD Power of around 15,000 purchasers of new 2012 to 2014 model-year vehicles reported that about 34 percent of automotive Internet users (defined as new-vehicle buyers who use the Internet when they shop) use either a tablet or smartphone while shopping at a dealership. Pricing information is the most frequently accessed information, at 61 percent, followed by model information (42 percent), searching inventory (40 percent), and special offers/incentives (36 percent). Of the people who use mobile devices to get vehicle-pricing information at a dealership, 84 percent leverage that information in the negotiations, and 73 percent have gotten a better deal as a result, according to the study.

Nearly 59 percent of the 14.4 hours spent buying a car involves researching and shopping online, according to the *2016 Car Buyer Journey*, a study commissioned by Cox Automotive through IHS Automotive. The study reinforced the need for dealers to focus on the overall buying experience just as much as they do on the product and the price. Jared Rowe, president of Cox Automotive Media, says, "Dealers have less than a 30 percent chance of changing a purchase decision once a customer is on the lot." He also says, "Today, car shopping is all about matchmaking—uniting sellers and buyers online. To create a perfect match, dealers should communicate a differentiator that represents their unique value so that consumers can identify the dealers that offer the specific car shopping experience they desire."

The findings of these studies are not surprising. The bottom line is that the Internet has made buyers much more educated when they buy cars. The vast amounts of data that are, literally, at the fingertips of potential buyers have leveled the playing field when these buyers cross the threshold of a dealership. However, the *2016 Car Buyer Journey* also reported that 71 percent of consumers said that they bought the vehicle they had first planned to buy when they visited a dealership. This favorable outcome is due to consumers who are so educated and armed with plenty of data that they could complete the purchase. However, it could be that these consumers at the dealership felt so entrapped in the process and Velcroed to their seat that they did not pursue their alternative—namely, leaving the dealership and buying a vehicle on more favorable terms elsewhere.

Finally, the *2016 Car Buyer Journey* reported that of the consumers who used the Internet to help them buy cars, 38 percent visited a single dealership and 52 percent drove only one vehicle. This data indicates that many of those consumers failed to consider their full range of buying options. The main frustrations of the buyers surveyed were filling out paperwork and negotiating the purchase or lease of the vehicle. What this tells me is that all the data in the world wouldn't help the buyer who is stressed or anxious about buying a car. You can prepare for the negotiation, but it might not play out exactly as scripted once you enter the dealership. As Mike Tyson famously said, "Everyone has a plan until they get punched in the mouth."

In the spirit of that comment, this book will not focus on the vast amount of data or extensive number of websites available to car buyers. You can have all the data you need and still fail when it's time for the negotiation. I can't tell you how many people prepare for the negotiation, arrive armed with plenty of data, and fail miserably in the negotiation. Instead, this book will provide you with a framework that will help you as you navigate through the negotiation.

So don't be anxious. Let the stress go away. The Rebel Negotiator is here to guide you through each step of the way.

CHAPTER

ONE

LET'S STICK TO THE RECIPE

When I ask workshop participants, "What does negotiation mean to you?" the feedback makes it appear as if I had asked about combat tactics. They generally describe negotiation as preparing for war—an adversarial process typically marked by screaming and yelling, fist pounding, trench warfare, and, ultimately, winning at all costs. As you prepare for your car dealership encounter, I encourage you to think of negotiation as a puzzle, not a battle. To help you change your point of view, I am giving you a recipe for becoming a successful negotiator. It has four key ingredients that must be properly mixed to achieve a "desirable" outcome. These are the ingredients: the ability to influence others; a strong mental and situational awareness; a methodology and process used in a principled and disciplined way; and a willingness to have a difficult conversation. Just like any other good recipe, it is both simple and complex, and usually requires fine-tuning to get it the final product just right.

"Desirable" in the car-buying context does not necessarily mean that you follow the recipe and drive the car home an hour later. As I like to say, negotiation, like life, is not always rainbows and lollipops. Getting that desirable outcome requires hard work, may take time, and is likely to force you to operate outside of your comfort zone.

Before I begin to explain each key ingredient, I must point out one thing: Pick an overall negotiation strategy that you will rely on as you venture out into the world of car buying. When thinking about such a strategy, think of the importance of what you are buying and the relationship you want to maintain with the other party to the negotiation.

A new car is a very significant purchase. Other than a house, it is likely to be one of the largest purchases you will make in your life. A new car also says a lot about who you are and how you want to be perceived—along with the size of your wallet, your family situation, your occupation, your personality type, your beliefs and attitudes, your aversion to change, your age, your gender, your education level, your desire for adventure, how much status you seek, and your level of education. Needless to say, there has been plenty of research in this area.

For that matter, the color of the car you buy also says a lot about your personality. For example, people who buy black cars tend to be aggressive and rebellious. And to put your mind at ease and feel comfortable about the legitimacy of my counsel as you enter these negotiations, I can tell you that the Rebel Negotiator has never owned anything other than black cars.

Now let me turn to the importance of the relationship that you want to maintain with the other parties, that is, the car salesperson and the dealership. At the risk of offending car salespeople, let me say that the public perception of their career is not very flattering—namely, a salesforce that consists of sleazy and tacky people who wear plaid jackets and are laden with gold chains. Most important, the one word most used to describe them is "untrustworthy." And that label has some truth to it. A 2014 Gallup poll asked, "[How would you] rate the honesty and ethical standards of people in these different fields—very high, high, average, low, or very low?"

The results, depicted in Figure 1 were based on the percentage of individuals who rated professions as highly or very highly ethical. They are as follows:

FIGURE 1

HONESTY & ETHICAL STANDARDS

Rating of honesty and ethical standards of people in these different fields—
very high, high, low or very low

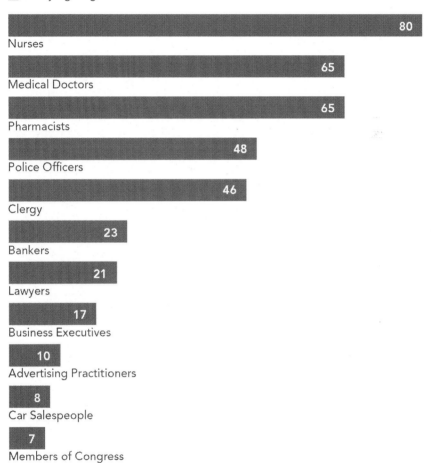

■ % Very high/High

Field	%
Nurses	80
Medical Doctors	65
Pharmacists	65
Police Officers	48
Clergy	46
Bankers	23
Lawyers	21
Business Executives	17
Advertising Practitioners	10
Car Salespeople	8
Members of Congress	7

Only 8 percent of survey respondents rated car salespeople as having high or very high ethical standards. Clearly, car salespeople have to work on their image. Why, Rebel Negotiator, are you sharing this information with us? you might ask. The answer is clear—you don't care about maintaining a relationship with a car salesperson or even a car dealership. They will always be there waiting to sell you a car or to charge you for service, no matter where you made your purchase. With that dynamic, you should never let your relationship with the car salesperson affect your buying decision. I will discuss the best alternative to a negotiated agreement (known as BATNA) later, but you will never have a stronger BATNA than when you are buying a car. The Rebel Negotiator will never worry about his relationship with a car salesperson, and the list of dealerships that he has left midnegotiation is very long. It is my hope and belief that you can emulate my behavior.

Let's confirm that your negotiation strategy is what is called transactional, where the subject (i.e., the car) is the key focus, and the relationship is less important and is negligible, at best. Now that you have your strategy, let's look at each key ingredient.

CHAPTER  TWO

YOU AGREE WITH ME, RIGHT?

Influence is the first ingredient in the recipe to becoming a successful negotiator. It is, in short, the ability to influence others. Influence is the ability to have an effect on the character, development, or behavior of someone or something. Negotiation is the exercise of influence and we do this every day. Daily negotiation could be tacitly coordinating who will enter a door or an elevator, interacting with the coffee barista or waiter to make sure that your drink or lunch is prepared the way you like it, or building a relationship with a family member. An important client negotiation takes into account the concerns of all parties. If you don't like to negotiate or don't believe you are good at it, I challenge you to think about how many times each day you successfully influence and "negotiate" with people around you.

How do you influence the car salesperson you are negotiating with to agree with what you believe or want? Your first choice may be to use logic to persuade the salesperson. Although logic may lead to a successful outcome, you should realize that you don't have much of a relationship with the car salesperson and the dealership, so they may not want to accept your logic as rational. If this happens, support your reasoning with an expert opinion, industry standard, or established precedent. If this doesn't work, tell them what you want to do, and leave it at that.

If this approach doesn't work, you could try to influence the other party with social options that may include socializing with that party or appealing to the relationship. By attempting to establish some level of affiliation with the car salesperson, you may get that party to agree or cooperate with you on issues in the negotiation. Although doing this may be a good option when you are likely to have a relationship with the party, it may not count for much when you're buying a car. You could decide to influence the car salesperson by trying to engage him in the process—in essence, to build them a golden bridge. A salesperson works on commission and won't be compensated if you head to the dealership down the street. If your influence and persuasion are not working, think of what Tom Cruise said in the movie *Jerry Maguire*: "Help me help you."

Also, if your efforts are unsuccessful, you can always use negative-influence techniques, including manipulation (lies and deceit), intimidation (loud and abrasive verbal aggressiveness), avoidance (doing nothing), or threats (comply with what I want, or else). These techniques, however, may mislead other parties or cause them to act against their best interests or wishes. If you want to use these techniques at the dealership, they would sound something like this:

Avoiding: "If you want to sell me the car for the price I am willing to pay, you know how to reach me. Have a nice day."

Manipulating: "I have called your competitor and they have agreed to sell me the car for $2,000 less than you, and they are giving me a more attractive price on my trade-in. I better leave now so I don't get caught in traffic."

Intimidating: "What kind of business do you run here? I can't believe how poorly you treat prospective customers. Your behavior in this entire sales process has been rude, disrespectful, and completely unacceptable." (Of course, say this loudly so it is heard by other customers. In addition, it may not hurt to gently pound your fist on the table before you say this.)

Threatening: "If you don't sell me the car for the price and terms I am demanding, I will tell all of my friends, family, and colleagues never to come to this dealership ever again. I will also make sure that my 47,000 Twitter followers, 1,248 LinkedIn Connections, and thousands of Facebook friends will never set foot in this dealership."

The influence ingredient of the successful negotiator recipe is extremely important. Depending on the situation, you can determine how to best influence the other party to agree with you. Hopefully, your approach to negotiation will use logic or social methods, but you can use negative-influence techniques, if needed.

CHAPTER  THREE

ARE YOU PAYING ATTENTION?

The second key ingredient in the recipe to becoming a successful negotiator is to stay very disciplined, and the best way to do that is by understanding the situation and how effective you are at the negotiating table. These variables are always in motion and they must be fine-tuned during the negotiation.

First, let's first talk about situational awareness, or spotting the game you're playing. "Spotting the game" is very important because it will dictate the outcome and success of the negotiation. Key questions asked in this game-spotting analysis are these:

1. Have the parties effectively defined the issues?

2. Have the parties clearly articulated their interests?

3. Have the parties considered the full range of options?

4. Have the parties used objective, measurable, and verifiable standards to develop the options?

5. Have the parties discussed their alternatives and what will happen if the parties can't reach an agreement?

6. Who is making commitments in the negotiation? Is it one-sided?

7. Is the relationship affecting the negotiation? Are any of the parties being manipulated?

8. How is the communication flow? Are the parties listening or talking past each other? Are they treating each other with respect? Are they attacking the issues or the people at the table?

When you have spotted the game, you can then decide if you want to continue playing the same game, if you want to change it, or if you want to stop playing altogether. Examples of games you don't want to play when buying a new car include bidding against yourself, bargaining that results in compromise, caving in because you feel heavily invested in the process, playing chicken, rewarding anchoring, or making decisions based on your perceived level of entrapment. The bottom line is that you should never react only to what the other side is doing.

Because it is important for you to have strong situational awareness and avoid participating in a game you don't want to play, I want to go through each of these following scenarios in detail.

Let's start with bidding against yourself. The buyer makes commitments and concessions with little or no feedback from the seller. If you've watched the TV show *Pawn Stars*, you know what this looks like. The dialogue in the car-buying context would sound something like this:

Buyer: I am interested in trading in my 2014 Mercedes-Benz E63S for a new 2018 model. My car is in like-new condition and has 10,500 miles. I have done some market research on the trade-in value for cars in similar condition and want $67,500 for the car.

Salesperson: That seems like quite a lot for that car.

Buyer: OK. How about $64,500?

Salesperson: That is a little more reasonable.

Buyer: How about $60,000?

Salesperson: Well, that is better, and we are pretty close.

Buyer: OK. The minimum I will accept is $55,000.

Salesperson: OK. Let me check with my sales manager.

Let's think about what happened in this negotiation for the car's trade-in value. The buyer has taken an 18 percent haircut for what he believed was market-relevant value for the car and the dealer has not yet made a commitment.

The only person making commitments in this exchange is the buyer. The sales manager, the party who has the power to make a commitment on behalf of the dealership, has not even joined the conversation. Here, the buyer needs to slow down and run through the eight questions I identified above. When buyers have asked those questions and have "spotted the game," they can adjust their approach accordingly. Figure 2 shows a diagram of what bidding against yourself looks like.

FIGURE 2

BIDDING AGAINST YOURSELF

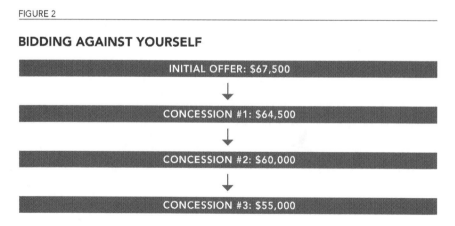

INITIAL OFFER: $67,500

↓

CONCESSION #1: $64,500

↓

CONCESSION #2: $60,000

↓

CONCESSION #3: $55,000

Now let's take a look at classic traditional bargaining that results in a compromise. If you are a fan of compromise, you should look carefully at its definition. Compromise is an agreement or a settlement of a dispute, which is reached by each side making concessions, to accept standards that are less than desirable. From the Rebel Negotiator's perspective, this is not a good result. I would much rather collaborate with the party on the other side of the table.

The dialogue for traditional bargaining would sound like this:

Buyer: I am interested in trading in my 2014 Mercedes-Benz E63S for a new 2018 model. My car is in like-new condition and has 10,500 miles. I have done some market research on the trade-in value for cars in similar condition and want $67,500 for the car.

Salesperson: That seems quite a lot for that car, but I can agree to $57,500.

Buyer: How about $65,000?

Salesperson: I can't agree to a penny over $59,000.

Buyer: What if we split the difference?

Salesperson: We are $6,000 apart, so that would be $62,000.

Buyer: OK. Let's do it for $62,000.

Salesperson: OK. $62,000 it is.

Even though this may seem like a reasonable result, it has created nothing but waste because it left both sides unhappy and dissatisfied. Did the parties even bother to discuss their interests or the range of satisfying options? Too often people want to "split the difference," and too often they leave plenty of waste on the table and end up feeling like the children in the story of Jack and Jill arguing over an orange. In that story, Jack and Jill are fighting over the last orange in the bowl. After they agree to split the orange in half, Jack takes his half, eats the fruit, and throws away the peel. Jill takes her half, throws away the fruit, and uses the peel to bake a cake. If Jack and Jill had simply discussed their interests, they would have used the entire orange. Instead, Jack's stomach is empty and Jill's cake is flavorless. When you are in the dealership and there is a disagreement over price, don't ever split oranges. Figure 3 shows traditional bargaining that results in a compromise.

FIGURE 3

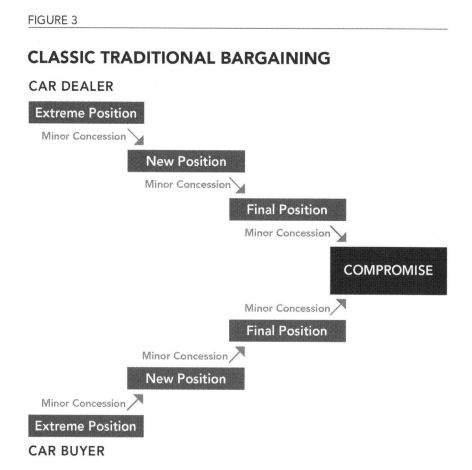

CLASSIC TRADITIONAL BARGAINING

CAR DEALER

Extreme Position
Minor Concession
New Position
Minor Concession
Final Position
Minor Concession
COMPROMISE
Minor Concession
Final Position
Minor Concession
New Position
Minor Concession
Extreme Position

CAR BUYER

Let's now focus on an oldie but goodie: caving in. Caving in happens when one party to the negotiation firmly holds on to a position during the negotiation. Based upon the passage of time, the investment of resources, or some other event, that same party magically decides to give up that position and agree to the other party's demand. I find caving in to be one of the most frustrating things that a party to a negotiation can do. Why bother holding on to a position when you intended to give in all along? Holding on to that position yielded nothing but wasted time and effort for both parties. Caving in is not a page in the Rebel Negotiator's playbook. If a position is important on Day 1 of the negotiation, it will be just as important on Day 30 or Day 300. Rebel Negotiators say what they mean and mean what they say. They will not waste a bunch of time trying to get the other party to search for options to meet their interest, only to say "it's OK ... just kidding" at the last minute.

Even though our negotiation with the car dealer may not last for 300 days, let's take a look at what caving in sounds like in the trade-in situation.

Buyer: I am interested in trading in my 2014 Mercedes-Benz E63S for a new 2018 model. My car is in like-new condition and has 10,500 miles. I have done some market research on the trade-in value for cars in similar condition and want $67,500 for the car.

Salesperson: That seems quite a lot for that car, but I can agree to $63,500.

Buyer: I have done my research and $67,500 is a legitimate and market-relevant price for my car, given its condition and mileage. I will not accept a penny less. This is a **deal breaker** for me.

Salesperson: Let me talk with the sales manager and see what I can do for you.

Buyer: OK, but to be clear, I will not accept anything less than $67,500.

Salesperson: I spoke with my manager and the best we can do is

$63,500. I am even giving up part of my commission at that price.

Buyer: Maybe you are not listening to me. I will not agree to anything less than $67,500.

Hours pass and it is now 8:00 p.m.

Salesperson: OK. I have done everything I can. I called the general manager and the owner of the dealership. The best price we can offer is $63,500. Is that acceptable?

Buyer: OK. I will agree to $63,500.

As you can see, this is an extremely frustrating set of circumstances. Why did you finally say "yes" after all this time of saying "no"? You should put your best foot forward in the negotiation. If $63,500 was an acceptable offer for the trade-in that satisfies your interests, then please just accept the offer. In this case, the offer could have been accepted early in the day and the deal could have been finalized with plenty of time left over for dinner and a bottle of wine. By continuing to say "no," you have done nothing but waste time and undermine the negotiation. Figure 4 shows caving in.

FIGURE 4

CAVING IN

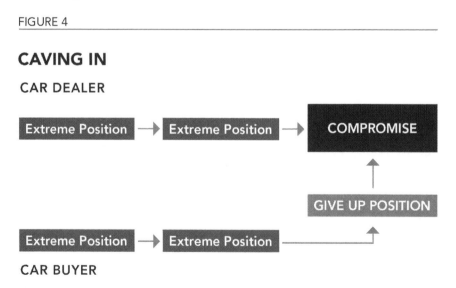

-24-

Now let's play chicken. This game typically involves two vehicles driven directly toward each other to test which driver will swerve away first. In the context of negotiation, playing chicken means the parties make mutual challenges or threats, hoping the other party will withdraw or acquiesce before a conflict or a collision occurs. Usually, this game reaches an impasse, forcing the parties to pursue an alternative. My advice is this: Never play chicken with a car dealer. Given the strength of your BATNA, there is no need to play such a dangerous game. Figure 5 shows a game of chicken.

FIGURE 5

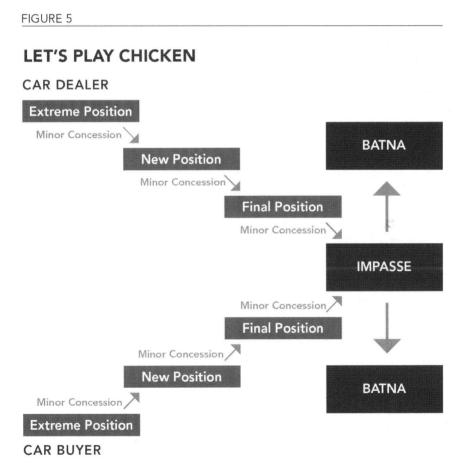

LET'S PLAY CHICKEN

So, you won't be playing chicken, but let me make sure that anchoring will not be rewarded. Anchoring happens when the opposing party sticks to its position while you provide offer after offer to move toward that position. Let's see what that sounds like when you are trying to get an acceptable price for the trade-in.

Buyer: I am interested in trading in my 2014 Mercedes-Benz E63S for a new 2018 model. My car is in like-new condition and has 10,500 miles. I have done some market research on the trade-in value for cars in similar condition and want $67,500 for the car.

Salesperson: I can offer only $58,000. That is my final offer.

Buyer: OK. How about $62,000?

Salesperson: No, the best I can do is $58,000. The car is not worth more than that.

Buyer: OK. I will come down to $60,000, but that is my best and final offer.

Salesperson: I appreciate the offer, but I simply can't do any better than $58,000.

Buyer: OK. Best and really final offer—$59,000. Come on. Work with me a little bit.

Salesperson: I have an idea. Let's split the difference and agree on $58,500.

Buyer: OK. You have a deal.

In this scenario, not only did the buyer reward the salesperson for anchoring to the initial $58,000 offer, but he added insult to injury by agreeing to split the difference. Ultimately, the seller agreed to a minor $500 concession, whereas the buyer reduced his original and market-relevant price by around 13 percent. We will not reward car salespeople for anchoring to their price that is not grounded in legitimacy. Here, you should wave goodbye to the salesperson as you walk out the door, and then drive to one of the dealership's competitors. Figure 6 shows a game of rewarding anchoring.

FIGURE 6

REWARDING ANCHORING

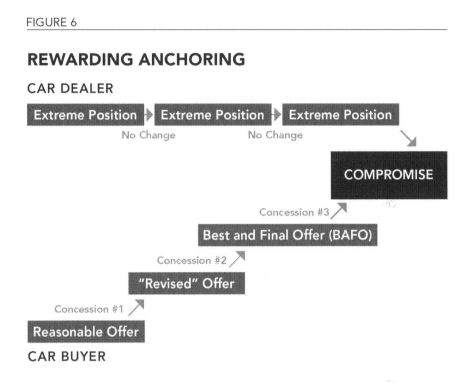

The last game that I want you to spot is entrapment. From the second you enter the car dealership, remember that you are free to say no and leave at any time. You are not detained, restrained, or kept in custody. Before you sit down and begin the negotiation, make a mental note of all the exits and be prepared to use them if you have to. Also, check your clothing and the chair you're sitting in, and make sure there's no Velcro.

Entrapment occurs when you enter the dealership and you really need to get a new car. Maybe you don't have a lot of time. Maybe you need to drive the car to an important event that evening. Maybe you can't live with the thought of not leaving in that shiny new whip. In each scenario, you are overwhelmed by the belief that you can't walk away because you have nowhere to walk to. As I will tell you time after time, you will never have a stronger BATNA in your life than when you enter a car dealership to trade in the old and purchase a new car—period. I don't care if you like the dealership, like the salesperson, love the car, like the free Otis Spunkmeyer cookies, or whatever your excuse: You will never be entrapped when buying a new car if you follow this rule. If you remember nothing else from this book, remember this key rule.

Now that you can spot the game, I'd like to discuss the importance of mental awareness when you're seated at the negotiation table. Ultimately, your level of success at the table and your method of engaging with others will be shaped by your social style, your personality type, and how you deal with conflict. No matter what, it is important to be a good listener, to inquire instead of advocate, to seek to understand instead of seeking to be understood, and to find the right balance between directness and diplomacy. Finally, before you sit at the negotiation table, ask yourself if you want to be right or to be effective.

One key component that will significantly affect your ability to be a successful negotiator is how you approach conflict. The Thomas-Kilmann Conflict Mode Instrument is a popular tool that assesses a person's behavior in conflict situations, in which the concerns of people appear to be incompatible. The instrument measures two factors: (1) assertiveness, the extent that the person attempts to satisfy the person's own concerns; and (2) cooperativeness, the extent that the person attempts to satisfy the other person's concerns. Ultimately, these behaviors can define five methods of dealing with conflict: competing, collaborating, compromising, avoiding, and accommodating. Figure 7 shows the types of conflict modes measured against the assertiveness and cooperativeness scales. Let me describe each method in more detail:

FIGURE 7

THOMAS-KILMANN CONFLICT MODE INSTRUMENT

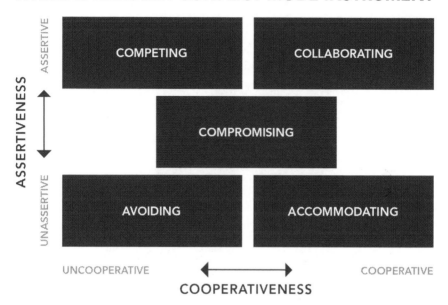

1. **Competitors:** A competitor is both assertive and uncooperative, and pursues his own interests at the expense of others. A competitor wants to win and will use whatever means are at his disposal to do so.

2. **Collaborator:** A collaborator is both assertive and cooperative. A collaborator attempts to find a solution that satisfies the interests of both parties.

3. **Compromiser:** A compromiser is midway between both assertiveness and cooperativeness. The compromiser tries to find an acceptable solution that partially satisfies the interests of both parties. As I previously discussed, compromisers like to split oranges.

4. **Avoider:** An avoider is both unassertive and uncooperative and, as the name indicates, avoids conflict completely.

5. **Accommodator**: An accommodator is the opposite of the competitor in that he neglects his own concerns to satisfy the concerns of the other party.

No one conflict-handling mode is best because each may be used depending on the circumstances. I will let you determine your social style, your personality type, and your style of approaching conflict, but I will give you high-level advice that you can use if your profile is strong in any one area.

1. **Competitors**: Ask more questions, be more flexible, decide if the relationship matters, and don't be overly confident in the strength of your alternative.

2. **Collaborators**: Focus on preparation and take the time to clearly understand the interests of both parties.

3. **Compromisers**: Don't split oranges. Don't accept the first acceptable answer, and be more creative.

4. **Avoiders**: Get help if necessary. Conflict is not a bad thing. You can disagree without being disagreeable.

5. **Accommodators**: Be more active in the negotiation. Don't be afraid to assert your interests and focus on objective criteria that support the reasonableness of those interests. Don't underestimate the strength of your alternative.

Even if your social style and personality type are so heavily ingrained in who you are that they cannot change, you can successfully temper your approach to conflict at the negotiation table. I speak from experience as an extremely competitive person: I've learned to temper my approach to conflict by keeping my competitive arousal in check and focusing on collaboration so I can be more effective at the negotiation table.

ARE YOU PAYING ATTENTION?

You will be competing at the highest level when you negotiate to buy a car. You will focus on your interests at the expense of others' and will use whatever means necessary to get the best possible price and best possible terms for the trade-in of your old car and purchase of the new one. You will be self-aware and will focus on your ultimate goal: driving that new car home.

As for self-awareness, it is important to find an appropriate balance between focusing on your interests at the expense of others' and winning at all costs. In their May 2008 *Harvard Business Review* article, "When Winning Is Everything," Deepak Malhotra, Gillian Ku, and J. Keith Murnighan suggested that the win-at-all-costs type of decision-making was driven by an "adrenaline-fueled emotional state," called competitive arousal. You can probably think of a time when you were a victim of competitive arousal and made a decision in the heat of battle that, in retrospect, looked foolish. Sometimes, you want to win at all costs, even if the decision-making process lacks sound judgment and is solely based on competitive arousal. To mitigate this win-at-all-costs dynamic, it is crucial that you stay disciplined at the negotiation table, keep in mind your ultimate goal, and manage your emotions. By taking this approach, you can keep in check competitive arousal, and you can breathe in that new-car smell.

CHAPTER  FOUR

MAINTAIN DISCIPLINE AND FOLLOW THE PROCESS

To be a successful negotiator, you must have a strict methodology that you use in every negotiation. That methodology is the third key ingredient in your recipe for becoming a successful negotiator after influence and mental and situational awareness. The first step is to identify your goal for the negotiation. If you don't know that, then you might as well call it a day and play golf. Once you have identified your goal, the next step is preparation. I strictly follow the approach that former New York Giants head Coach Tom Coughlin shared during a press conference before Super Bowl XLVI—humble enough to prepare, confident enough to perform.

As you prepare, remember that the negotiation may not flow as smoothly as it did when you role-played in the mirror or with your friends, family, or office colleagues. In the words of the great philosopher and pugilist Mike Tyson: "Everyone has a plan till they get punched in the mouth." As long as you can spot the game and use the methodology I will discuss, the punch should leave you unfazed and ready for more action.

Let's assume that you have reined in your competitive arousal, you clearly know your goal, you have prepared diligently, and you are about to begin negotiating. The key question is: How do you reach an agreement that meets your interests and is acceptable to the car dealership? My answer has been the same for many years and has served me well in the marketplace: 4x7. This approach has four key principles and seven elements, and, frankly, is easy to understand. If you can master 4x7, then you are well on your way to becoming a very successful negotiator. These are the four principles:

1. Temper your approach based upon the amount of risk in the outcome. (Will you consider a preowned car? A dealer demo model? A different color, model, or set of options?)

2. Temper your approach based on the relevant geography. (How you approach the salesperson in New York may be different from how you approach the salesperson in Omaha.)

3. Temper your approach based upon the person sitting across from you at the negotiation table. (In a car dealership, this is likely to be the salesperson as well as the sales manager.)

4. Remember that conflicts are created, conducted, and sustained by human beings, and can be resolved by human beings. (It's just a new car—no need to get overly stressed or anxious.)

Principle 4 is a recent addition to the list (a list that I had not changed in 15 years, so this was a big deal). The addition came from a 2010 speech by former U.S. Senate Majority Leader George Mitchell, who had just been named as a special envoy to the Middle East, a very critical and challenging role. After being introduced at the appointment ceremony, Mitchell said: "Conflicts are created, conducted, and sustained by human beings, and can be resolved by human beings." I am in no way comparing buying a car to negotiating peace in the Middle East, but you should keep the scope of the negotiation in perspective throughout the process.

The 4x7's seven-element approach in a principled negotiation stems from the book *Getting to Yes,* by Roger Fisher and William Ury of the

Harvard Negotiation Project. The seven elements are interests, options, legitimacy, alternatives, commitment, communication, and relationship. The key to success is your ability to identify these elements and how they connect, and, most important, to understand how they evolve during a negotiation. As I previously discussed, it is also absolutely critical that you take the time to prepare for any negotiation and carefully consider how the seven elements can affect it. If you have not prepared properly, you might as well cancel the meeting because the result will not be good. Remember Coach Coughlin's approach: humble enough to prepare, confident enough to perform. I say: Learn it, know it, and live it.

While I am quoting people, take a look at what Harvey Specter, the lawyer in the television show *Suits*, said: "What are your choices when someone puts a gun to your head? . . . What are you talking about? You do what they say or they shoot you. WRONG. You take the gun, or you pull out a bigger one. Or, you call their bluff. Or, you do one of a hundred and forty-six other things." Remember that you are in the driver's seat (no pun intended) and your BATNA is extremely strong (you have many places to walk to) in negotiating the price and terms of a new car. The list of car dealerships that the Rebel Negotiator has walked out of is long and distinguished, and it is likely you will do this as you navigate through negotiations. But it's OK—take a deep breath, get up from your chair, put one foot in front of the other, head out the door, and drive away.

Ultimately, these seven elements dictate your likelihood of success in any negotiation as well as the final words in the sales agreement. How these elements are interconnected is demonstrated in the negotiation, whose desired goal is reaching an agreement that satisfies the mutual interests of the parties. If an option is identified that meets those interests, then there's a clear path forward; if not, then the parties may have to pursue their alternatives, also known—as I have previously mentioned—as their best alternative to a negotiated agreement (BATNA). As I like to say, negotiation is that simple and that complex. Let's revisit those seven elements, in more detail:

1. **Interests:** What are the needs, concerns, goals, hopes, and fears that are motivating the other party to negotiate?

2. **Options:** What approaches can be identified that meet the mutual interests of the parties?

3. **Legitimacy:** What criteria exist—industry practices, expert opinions, laws, rules or regulations, or precedent—to measure if the options considered or agreement reached is fair and sensible?

4. **Alternatives:** What unilateral steps can either party take—how can their interests be satisfied elsewhere—if the parties can't reach an agreement?

5. **Commitment:** Is the other party prepared to reach an agreement and does the party have the power to do it?

6. **Communication:** Are the parties collaborating by listening and talking to each other, and remaining unconditionally constructive?

7. **Relationship:** Do I care about maintaining a relationship with the party across the table?

The focus on and the benchmark for success should be an agreement that does this:

- Satisfies the interests of the parties

- Minimizes waste and reflects the best of many options

- Neither party feels taken advantage of by the option chosen

- Is better than your best alternative, or BATNA

- Embodies a commitment among the parties

- Is grounded in open communication

- Reinforces the relationship between the parties

Your ability to spot the seven elements will very much help you execute an agreement. Figure 8 shows an overall view of the seven elements.

FIGURE 8

7 ELEMENTS

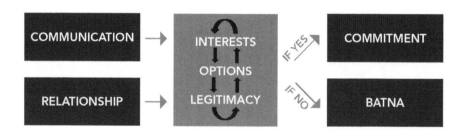

You can read lots of books and attend plenty of trainings on successful negotiation techniques and tactics. However, I assure you that if you strictly follow the four core principles and keep a laser focus on the seven elements, you will make great strides in the art of negotiation.

I will now review the other principles at the core of negotiation. What does it mean to temper your negotiation approach based upon the amount of risk in the outcome? As I previously discussed, you should consider a variety of factors in measuring such risk. Risk factors that impact the outcome may include buying a preowned vehicle, accepting a dealer demonstrator, buying a vehicle that is a different color or is equipped differently from you had originally thought of, accelerating the timeline of your purchase, agreeing to different financing terms, or buying a completely different make and model than what you had planned. What will the impact of these decisions be on performance, your finances, your warranty, and, most of all, your level of happiness?

According to the second principle, it is important to temper your approach based upon your geographic region. What works well in New York or San Francisco might not work well in New Orleans or Dallas. Before jumping into the negotiation, you must understand not only the local laws (yes, they can vary as they relate to the lease or purchase of a new car) but also the effect that culture may have on the negotiation. Is the style quiet and less flamboyant, requiring some level of deference, or louder and more aggressive? I will tell you: Prepare and temper your approach accordingly.

Finally, remember to temper your style and approach based upon the person sitting across from you at the negotiation table. Although you can study countless books on negotiation tactics, I urge you to make every attempt to understand the style, personality, motivation, emotions, and interests of the person with whom you will be negotiating. Ultimately, your success hinges on your ability to work with that person to reach an agreement with an acceptable level of risk and reward for the parties to the transaction.

I would like to introduce you to the "Harley Principle." I have been riding Harley-Davidson motorcycles for the past 18 years, and it is a great passion of mine. I have a V-Rod and a Screamin' Eagle Springer, and love the feeling of rolling down the road with the wind in my face on a beautiful summer day. If I enter the office of the person I will be negotiating with and see anything Harley-Davidson or motorcycle related, I always ask about it, and the conversation quickly shifts to a passion we both share.

Finding this common interest lets you to identify with each other in a way that transcends the pricing, terms and conditions, and adversarial negotiations that you are about to undertake. Although I am not suggesting that a common passion for Harley-Davidson motorcycles results in an easy negotiation, it allows me to identify with the person I'm dealing with. Even though I have no scientific evidence, I can absolutely tell you that my negotiations with motorcycle enthusiasts over the years have been very successful. So, make an effort to identify with the party you'll be negotiating with over and above the terms and conditions in the agreement; it definitely will make a difference.

CHAPTER

FIVE

THIS IS NOT GOING TO BE PLEASANT

The final ingredient in the recipe for becoming a successful negotiator is the ability to have a difficult conversation. As we all know, negotiations are not always focused on rainbows and lollipops, and as President John F. Kennedy said: "Let us never negotiate out of fear. But let us never fear to negotiate." You must be ready, willing, and able to engage in a difficult conversation.

Your comfort level in doing this will be tightly connected to how you approach conflict. Competitors will be ready to jump right in as they want to win at all costs. For avoiders, having a difficult conversation is like having a root canal.

Sometimes the difficult conversation causes stress and anxiety because you have a relationship with the other party. Delivering a difficult message to a party whom you want to maintain a relationship with is much more challenging than one where the level of engagement is business only, at best. The conversation with the car salesperson falls into the business only category, so preparing for the difficult conversation ("I am buying from another dealer, I am leaving now, or I don't trust what you are telling me") should not cause too much angst.

To build a level of comfort for a difficult conversation, I recommend that you take these four key steps:

1. **Be prepared.** Preparation is an absolute necessity for any negotiation and even more so for delivering a difficult message. I can't stress enough the importance of thorough preparation. Make sure that you have an in-depth understanding of the issues and that you focus on legitimacy. If necessary, you can role-play the negotiation with a friend or colleague.

2. **Seek to understand instead of seeking to be understood.** The difference may seem subtle, but it is significant and will affect the tone and tenor of your conversation. Use inquiry instead of advocacy, and find the right balance between diplomacy and directness.

3. **Prepare yourself for a negative reaction.** The conversation may become tense. Your preparation should help you become emotionally ready. Keep your competitive arousal in check—ask yourself, do you want to be right or to be effective?

4. **Keep things in perspective.** How significant are the message and the issue? Will it even matter in six months? In six years?

CHAPTER

SIX

THE 7 ELEMENTS IN ACTION

Now that you have the recipe for becoming a successful negotiator, let's think about how you can perfect it for your new-car purchase. I will conduct an in-depth analysis of each of the seven elements, but let's look at the overall approach.

When you sit down at the negotiating table, your ultimate objective should be to strive for an effective and efficient negotiation. To be effective, you should communicate in an open, honest, and candid manner with the other party. To do this, I strongly urge you to focus on your ability to listen carefully. A good acronym to remember to help you do this is to be a good LIAR—[L]isten, [I]nquire, [A]cknowledge, and [R]espond. I encourage you to seek to understand instead of seeking to be understood, and use inquiry instead of advocacy. Do not talk past each other. It is amazing how much you can learn by slowing down, listening, and asking questions. The other element of an effective negotiation is to maintain a good working relationship with the other party. For the competitors out there, I recommend that you establish a level of affiliation—even if it is at a basic and superficial level—with your counterpart. By doing this, you will see that person in a more human light and be more inclined to collaborate.

For efficiency, I strive for a negotiation that will allow me to make the best and most informed decision; I will not accept a bad result because I am either emotional or wedded to my position. To help you make the best and most informed decision possible, the seven-element model focuses on the relevant interests of the parties. You must be cognizant of the interests of both parties. Then you can develop options, one of which will, hopefully, satisfy those interests and allow the parties to reach an agreement and make a commitment. The hope is that the mutually acceptable option is grounded in legitimacy (it is fair and reasonable and has been tested against market standards) and is better than each party's alternative.

I urge you to take as much time as necessary to think carefully about the full range of options that may satisfy the interests of the parties. When you think you have exhausted the potential options, think again. Be open to considering all options; rather than saying no, think about under what conditions you might say yes.

Your intent once you cross the threshold of the dealership is to engage in an effective and efficient negotiation. It will be successful if you negotiate in a way that achieves these goals:

- Satisfies the interests of the parties and does not create waste

- Results in the best of many options

- Grounded in legitimacy and fairness

- Better than your best alternative

- Memorialized in a well-planned commitment

- Built on a foundation of good communication

- Follows a process that improves the working relationship

THE 7 ELEMENTS IN ACTION

Now that you have a basic understanding of the seven-element process, I will thoroughly review each element and how it will affect your car-buying experience.

CHAPTER

SEVEN

RELATIONSHIP—CAN'T WE ALL JUST GET ALONG?

If I were giving you general advice in the spirit of achieving an effective negotiation, I would strongly recommend that you build a good working relationship with the other party you're negotiating with. My advice would apply even if the interaction is purely transactional. As you can tell, the Rebel Negotiator does not avoid conflict; his Thomas-Kilmann compete score is off the chart. That approach has earned him another nickname: Bulldog.

But there are times when the Bulldog must stay in the cage to be effective. A key component of being a successful negotiator is to find a way to humanize the adversarial process by establishing an affiliation with the person you are negotiating with. Then you will be able to see your adversary in a more human light and your desire to collaborate with that person should increase. Even if such affiliation is, at best, only superficial, it is an extremely important part of the negotiation. However, in buying your new car, I want you to forget that advice completely.

I have nothing against car salespeople, sales managers, or anyone else you may encounter in the dealership hierarchy when you are negotiating the value of your trade-in and the purchase of your new car. I am sure they are all nice people and I encourage you to make friends with them in any social capacity you deem appropriate. But once you walk into the dealership, you must stick to this rule: You are not here to build relationships with anyone and will not let any relationship—real, perceived, or otherwise—influence your decision-making. If you might find that perspective overly aggressive or unfriendly, I would ask you these questions:

1. How often do you buy a new car? Do you think it will matter in two, four, or five years, what, if any, relationship you built with the salesperson?

2. What is the probability that the salesperson you purchase this car from will even be around when it is time for the next purchase? The 2015 National Automobile Dealers Association annual *Dealership Workforce Study* reported that sales consultant turnover is 71.9 percent a year.

3. Even if you build a relationship, what level of authority does the salesperson have over price and terms?

4. Other than nominal concessions, such as a detail or an extra set of floor mats, what special treatment or incentives have you received based upon having an excellent and ongoing relationship with your salesperson?

5. Given the level of competitiveness in the industry, do you really think the dealership will turn you away if you don't seek BFF status with its sales personnel?

6. What do you think the relationship will get you? Will it yield a candid, honest, and straightforward conversation? Are you going to be entitled to better prices or better terms?

I am not suggesting that you be impolite, avoid small talk, or refuse the soda, water, or cookies. I want to make sure that you see the level of engagement with the car salesperson for what it is. This sales professional is no more than an intermediary between you and the dealership to help along your transaction. I will talk about authority and commitment later, but it is important to remember just how much influence the salesperson actually has on the negotiation. Generally, he can't make decisions about the value of the trade-in; that is usually handled by the used-car department. He can't make decisions about the financing terms and conditions; that is handled by the finance department. He can't even make decisions about the sales price of the new car; that authority is with the new-car sales manager. The Rebel Negotiator bypasses the salesperson completely and asks to negotiate directly with the sales manager of the dealership. That way, I make it clear that I am not here to make friends but rather to buy a car.

If you still want to build a relationship, you can, but please remember to separate that relationship from the substance of the negotiation.

CHAPTER  EIGHT

COMMUNICATION—I'M SORRY, I DON'T UNDERSTAND YOU

Even though I might not care about building or maintaining a relationship with my car salesperson, it is important that I can communicate with him in a clear, concise, and efficient manner. I can't stress enough the importance of listening to the other party and seeking to understand instead of seeking to be understood. So often in a negotiation, the parties find themselves talking past the other party and hear only their position, and not the interests behind it. Disciplined negotiators listen for the interests behind those positions, and the standards the other party is using to support his perspective. Remember that at a basic level, negotiation is a task of influence. If I am going to be able to influence the other party, I need to understand the party's interests as deeply as possible so I can generate options that will address those interests and, hopefully, lead to a better agreement.

I encourage a very direct and firm approach to the salesperson—say what you mean and mean what you say. Again, there is no reason to stay at the dealership for the entire day and waste time. Prepare, prepare, and prepare again. Know the price you are willing to pay for the vehicle and the price you will accept for your trade in. I am not suggesting it has to be an absolute amount, but you should have a predetermined acceptable price range before you walk into the dealership. I advise you to tell the salesperson a firm number and let him know that if the dealership wants your business, then that is the price you are willing to accept. If not, then head out the door. In terms of the exact amount or the acceptable price range, a colleague suggests not using round numbers. He believes that communicating an exact number, namely, "I will pay $47,263," is more effective and reflects significant diligence in preparing the offer. I have no scientific evidence to support his claim, so I will leave this to your discretion.

There are buying services that claim they can get the best possible price for your car and bypass all communication and negotiation with the dealership. I am not a proponent of these services as they are not familiar with your interests and therefore could bind you to a suboptimal price and terms. You should conduct your own due diligence to determine how much you are willing to pay for your car and how much you expect for your trade-in. Once you have done your due diligence and decided on the vehicle you want to purchase, I encourage you to call the dealership and speak to a salesperson.

Tell the salesperson about the model of vehicle you are interested in buying and find out if it is in the inventory. If so, tell him how much you are willing to pay and that you are coming to the dealership only if the salesperson agrees to those terms. For example, say, "I am willing to pay invoice price for the vehicle." If you think that might be aggressive, you would be amazed at how many dealerships will accept that offer because they are still reaching their profitability targets from dealer-installed accessories, manufacturer holdbacks, extended warranties, advertising fees, document fees, appearance protection service contracts (wheel and tire protection, windshield replacement, and paintless dent repair), and other incentives they will realize for selling in-stock inventory in the current month.

I will get into the purchase details later, but I will say that all communication should be direct, firm, and unemotional. Tell the salesperson about your interests and the parameters you require to reach an agreement. If he agrees, then be ready, willing, and able to immediately execute the agreement. If he does not, move on to the next call.

CHAPTER  NINE

HOW EXACTLY IS THIS GAME PLAYED?

Before I discuss interests and consider options, I will talk about the financial fundamentals of buying cars. The easiest way for me to educate you is with frequently asked questions:

1. **What is the invoice price of a car?** The invoice price, or dealer cost, is the price on the invoice that the manufacturer sends to the dealer when the dealer receives a car from the factory. It includes the cost of the model of the vehicle plus the cost of any options and destination fees (the cost to transport the vehicle from the factory to the dealership). It may also include a standard advertising or marketing fee. Make sure that amount is reasonable. Given the pervasive use of holdbacks (see No. 5, below), it is important to know that the dealership may be paying less than the price on the invoice.

2. **What is the manufacturer's suggested retail price ("MSRP")?** The MSRP is exactly what it says, namely, the price the manufacturer suggests that the dealer should charge for the car. Know that this is a "suggested" price; the dealer can charge whatever price it deems appropriate.

3. **What about the sticker price I see on the windshield of a new car?** The sticker price is the amount that the dealer wants to get for the car. It may be the MSRP or may be marked up or down, depending upon the vehicle.

4. **What is the base or cash price?** The base or cash price is the price that you pay for the vehicle and will be in the sales contract.

5. **What is dealer holdback?** Dealer holdback is an amount paid to the dealer (anywhere from 2 percent to 3 percent) by the manufacturer for each new vehicle sold. It is calculated as a percentage of the invoice price or the MSRP (including or excluding options) or as a fixed amount. The dealer holdback allows a dealer to sell a car at less than the MSRP, or even at the invoice price, and still meet its profitability targets. The holdback is generally paid to the dealer as a rebate after the car has been sold. It is called a holdback because these funds are held back by the manufacturer and released only after the vehicle is sold.

6. **What is the average dealer markup?** The average dealer markup (the variance between the invoice price and sticker price) is typically between 2 percent and 5 percent, but can be substantially more (more than 10 percent) on luxury vehicles.

7. **How much commission will the car salesperson make on the sale?** Commission plans will vary depending upon the salesperson, the dealership, the geography, and the manufacturer, but a general benchmark is that the salesperson will make anywhere from 25 percent to 30 percent of the dealer's profit on the sale. Profit is defined as the difference between the selling price and the invoice price.

8. **What is a factory-to-dealer incentive?** Factory-to-dealer incentives are cash incentives that reduce the dealer's actual cost to buy the vehicle from the factory. These incentives may be offered on a geographic-specific or other basis to generate sales of specific models.

9. **How do I calculate a dealer's actual cost on a vehicle?** Actual Dealer Cost equals Factory Invoice minus Holdback minus Factory-to-Dealer Incentives.

10. **How do I calculate the dealer's profit on a vehicle?** Dealer Profit equals Retail Sales Price minus Factory Invoice plus Dealer Holdback plus Dealer Incentives.

CHAPTER

TEN

INTERESTS—I WANT IT MY WAY

Now that you have a general understanding of the financial mechanics of buying a car, let's discuss interests. At an overall level, interests are defined as the needs, concerns, goals, hopes, and fears that motivate parties to negotiate. To be successful in any negotiation, you must clearly document the interests of the parties, identify any interests that are shared, different, or in conflict, and analyze priorities. Most important, you must focus on interests and not positions. In discussing interests with the other party, here are general guidelines for success:

1. Prioritize the interests of the other party—don't assume you know what the party wants or needs.

2. Ask for tradeoffs among the various interests instead of trying to force your interests on the other party.

3. Prepare as diligently as possible.

4. Use inquiry to your advantage—do not advocate.

5. Listen carefully—seek to understand.

INTERESTS—I WANT IT MY WAY

As I discussed previously, positions are statements of what a party will or will not do, and are conclusions that are formed before the negotiation even begins. Positions are focused on satisfying the interests of one party and result in the other party reacting in one of two ways—fight or flight. Fighters say it is my way or the highway, which often leads to games of chicken with disastrous and undesirable results. Those who choose the flight option leave the table and pursue their alternative.

Good negotiators make every effort to understand the interests of all parties. However, less successful negotiators fight over positions, quickly reach an impasse, and either walk away from the table or reach a flawed agreement. These negotiators are so focused on position that they haven't taken the time to fully understand the interests of the other party. They approach the negotiation as haggling over opening positions, fighting to reach the best and final positions, and playing a game of concessions that is likely to result in "splitting the difference" and leaving plenty of waste on the table.

When you are trading in the old car and purchasing the new one, your interests are clear. You want to get the new car you want equipped the way you want it, to pay as little as possible for it (or, at a minimum, stay within your budget), to receive as much as possible on the trade-in (at a minimum, get a market-value amount and, if relevant, enough to pay off any note), and to engage in a quick, hassle-free transaction.

Although you will not fully understand the dealer's interests until you cross its threshold, you can expect its interests to be these: to sell the new car for the highest price possible (or, at a minimum, an amount that meets its profit objective); to offer as little as possible for the trade-in (or, at a minimum, an amount that will meet its profit objective when it offers the car for resale); to maintain a long-term customer relationship; and to move vehicles out of inventory. As a buyer, you should be aware of this inventory turnover interest because dealerships finance the purchase of their new-car inventories, and the more quickly they move inventory, the lower the monthly interest or carrying costs are. I advise starting and ending the negotiation during the last week of the month as dealers will be motivated to reduce month-end inventory levels.

It is also important to consider the interests of the salesperson and determine if his interests are consistent with the dealership's. Although he shares a broad interest in selling cars, the salesperson is likely to have a key interest in maximizing and accelerating his commission payments (he gets paid based on sales and not when customers walk away) and that interest may conflict with the sales manager's or dealership's interests in profitability. Many of these interests conflict with each other. You will need to prioritize the interests of the other party in the negotiation, identify shared interests, and develop options for those shared interests. According to Autodata Corporation, about 17.55 million cars were sold in the United States in 2016, so finding those shared interests and solving the car buying negotiation puzzle can be done.

Although I advocate identifying shared interests, you are going to be in compete mode when you enter the dealership. You are going to focus on developing an option that satisfies your interests well and that satisfies the interests of the dealer in an acceptable or tolerable way. Forget about win-win and smiles all around the table. Those can be saved for transactions in which you are not involved.

CHAPTER  ELEVEN

OPTIONS—UNDER WHAT CONDITIONS MIGHT YOU SAY YES?

Developing options is a crucial, if not the most important, component of being a successful negotiator. It is important to keep an open mind, to think outside the box, to wear your creative hat, and to stick to this principle: Rather than saying no, under what conditions might you say yes? As for the open-mind concept, it's important not to get too attached to a particular option, especially one you are most comfortable with based upon precedent. Just because you've been doing something a particular way for a long time doesn't mean it's not incredibly stupid.

Options are possible ways to satisfy the interests of the parties. The measuring stick for evaluating an option is whether it will result in an agreement that leaves no joint benefits on the table, is the best of many options, and meets everyone's interests (at some level). It is not simply splitting the difference. Remember that options (unlike alternatives, which are things you do away from the table—where you go when you walk away) are ideas on the table, with your bottom line being the least acceptable option that you would accept.

When you are in doubt, I want you to think about little Jack and Jill who were arguing over the orange. They agreed to split the orange and in doing so created nothing but an undesirable agreement with unrealized benefits. Had they taken the time to understand each other's interests, they could have invented an option for their mutual gain. So please, under no circumstance should you ever agree to split oranges. Let's take a look at how that might sound in the dealership:

Buyer: I will agree to pay $42,000 for the car.

Salesperson: Well, that is simply too low and my manager will never agree to that. The sticker price is $45,000 and the invoice price is $42,000. We can't sell you the car at invoice price because we will not be making any profit.

Buyer: Well, I know you are receiving holdback from the manufacturer and will still make a reasonable profit, even if you sell me the car at invoice price. So I am firm at $42,000.

Salesperson: Let me go and check with my manager. Twenty minutes passes.

Salesperson: I spoke with my manager and the lowest price he will agree to is $44,000.

Buyer: Well, I am at $42,000. What do you say we simply split the difference and agree to $43,000.

Salesperson: OK. Let me check with him.

A few minutes pass.

Salesperson: OK. We have a deal at $43,000.

In this scenario, the buyer clearly did some homework. The buyer knew the invoice price of the car as well as that the dealer was going to receive a holdback from the manufacturer, so the buyer knew the dealer would have gotten a reasonable profit margin by selling the car at the invoice price. However, the buyer and the salesperson set aside legitimacy and agreed to split oranges. The buyer paid an additional $1,000 for the car and did nothing but pad the dealer's profit. They did not spend any time discussing legitimate options—free maintenance, appearance protection service contracts (wheel and tire protection, windshield replacement, and paintless dent repair), or other services. If the parties had addressed these options, they could have dealt with the price variation and could have gotten real value. The buyer, however, rushed to judgment to his detriment and did not even think about pursuing his alternative. The buyer could have very easily gotten up out of the chair and left the dealership. If the buyer knew that $42,000 was a market-relevant and legitimate price for the car, then why deviate from that number?

How many times have you been involved in a negotiation where you believe you have deadlocked with the other party? Have you felt trapped with no apparent way forward? This is the turning point in a negotiation when you will either act like an inexperienced negotiator and compromise or split the difference, leaving both parties unhappy or dissatisfied. Or, you can act like a principled, disciplined, and experienced negotiator by refusing to haggle like fishmongers and, consequently, break the deadlock. To do so, you will seek out the interests behind the parties' positions. You will think creatively to identify new possibilities and new concepts grounded in legitimacy. Then you should be able to identify an option that will optimize both parties' outcomes or at least improve one party's well-being without harming the other. After doing that, you should be able to move forward to an agreement.

In buying a new car and trading in your old car, the options are extensive because the dealership is likely to look at the trade-in and new-car purchase as a portfolio with two components. If you can't reach an agreement because the price you want to pay for the new car is not acceptable to the dealership (too low) and the price it wants to give for your trade-in is not acceptable to you (also too low), then you can consider the following options:

1. If the trade-in offer is too low, you can accept the amount in exchange for a services or parts credit that can be used for future transactions. The dealership

may be inclined to agree to such a credit, given its cost to provide these services.

2. Accept the lower trade-in value but in exchange for not making payments on the new car for the first two or three months. This is a good option if the car will be financed through the manufacturer's financing entity, e.g., BMW Financial Services.

3. Propose a counteroffer to the trade-in value proposed by the dealership. That offer should be grounded in legitimacy (market value for cars in similar condition and similarly equipped).

4. The seller may attempt to offer other incentives in its control instead of continuing to negotiate the sales or trade-in price. That could include appearance protection service contracts, extended maintenance, free full detail services, or an extended warranty.

5. The dealer may manipulate the portfolio—offer more for the trade and less for the new purchase price, or vice versa. Pay attention to any benefit you'll get from this option. The dealer is robbing Peter to pay Paul, and any benefit you receive in this scenario is marginal, at best.

6. The dealer may agree to accept the higher offer for the trade-in or the lower price for the new car, and make it up on buyers who have not read this book.

7. As for the new car price, you can agree to pay a slightly higher price if the new car is limited in availability.

8. If you can't agree on the trade-in value, you can focus on the new-car purchase price first and leave the trade-in for later in the discussion. Or, you may decide to

unbundle the transaction and pursue your alternative on the trade-in (sell it on your own, take it elsewhere, or give it to a friend or family member).

9. Agree to a higher purchase price in exchange for more favorable financing terms, including a lower interest rate or term.

10. Agree to a higher purchase price in exchange for free maintenance over the warranty term.

11. Agree to a higher purchase price in exchange for free valet (pickup and delivery from your home or office) service while you own the car.

12. Agree to a higher purchase price in exchange for an extended warranty.

13. Propose looking at the Kelley Blue Book or some other price guide, and agreeing to let that guide set the final word (and serve as legitimacy) on setting the price.

14. Propose bringing in a friend or family member who also wants to purchase a new car and buy in bulk to receive a more attractive price.

15. Check if you qualify for affinity program discounts— AAA, American Bar Association, AARP—or other discounts you may be eligible for through your employer or otherwise.

16. In the spirit of the relationship, tell the salesperson that you will be back to purchase your next vehicle from him in a few months. That could appeal to his personal interests and generate goodwill that would result in a more favorable price.

17. Tell the salesperson that you will recommend him to your friends and family. That could also appeal to his personal interests and result in a more favorable price.

18. If the dealership is trying to focus on monthly payment amounts, turn the discussion to the purchase price for the vehicle. Don't be misled by a low monthly payment; it, generally, is too good to be true.

19. Inquire if there are other model vehicles from the same manufacturer that may have a more attractive purchase price or additional incentives. Or ask if a similar vehicle is in current inventory and may be equipped differently but may be available at a more attractive price.

There are, of course, many other options you can consider, depending on the vehicle, the dealership, the time of month, and the parties you are engaged with. Please note that you should consider only options that have a potentially higher purchase price if you are receiving something substantial in return.

Finally, the list above lacks alternatives you may pursue when you and the dealer can't agree on terms and conditions. Remember that options happen at the table; alternatives happen away from the table. I will discuss alternatives later in this book, but know that your alternatives are always very strong when you're trying to buy a new car.

CHAPTER  TWELVE

LEGITIMACY—IN GOD WE TRUST ... ALL OTHERS BRING DATA

Legitimacy is defined as how much an agreement is fair, wise, or sensible as measured by objective, measurable, and verifiable criteria. The first component of any successful negotiation is preparation. No matter how many cars you have bought, remember the words of former New York Giant's Coach Tom Coughlin: humble enough to prepare, confident enough to perform. Overall, legitimacy may include researching industry practices, expert opinions, laws, rules, regulations, precedent (in general and historically between the parties), standard procedures, and community standards.

Although the Rebel Negotiator believes that each element in a negotiation is important, legitimacy ranks at the top of the list. Think about positions and interests. It is very easy to establish a subjective one-sided position not grounded in reality well before the negotiation even begins. As I pointed out, positional negotiation quickly ends in fight or flight, neither of which is ideal. If the parties can identify interests and generate options, those options must be legitimate. If the other party refuses to negotiate fairly, the encounter is likely to be brief.

Unlike a salary negotiation where the result is highly ambiguous, the purchase of a new car and the value of a trade-in have clear guardrails. Think about it: You know the sticker price of the vehicle, and you have asked for and will see the invoice that has the price the dealer paid. You now know about holdback practices, so quick math will tell you exactly how much the dealer paid for the car you want to buy. You will also have plenty of the data from Internet searches that will tell you what similar buyers have paid for similar vehicles in your area. So before you even step into the dealership, you have a strong understanding of the zone of potential agreement (ZOPA) of the parties. This zone is the space between your bottom line (the last option you will accept before you go to your alternative) and the dealership's bottom line (the last option it will accept before it goes to its alternative). The zone of potential agreement is illustrated in Figure 9.

FIGURE 9

HOW WIDE IS THE ZOPA?

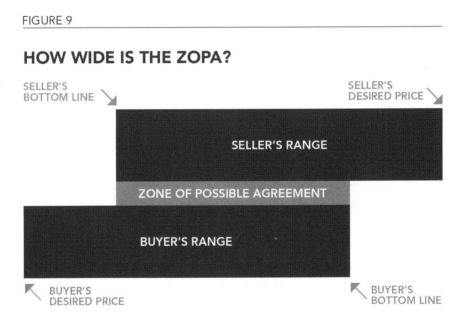

Each party's bottom line will be determined by the party's interests, the options that meet those interests, and legitimacy. In the car-buying context, legitimacy is based on the objective, measurable data from these sources:

1. **The Kelley Blue Book**: Collects its information from auctions throughout the country where cars' conditions are evaluated: excellent (looks new and is in excellent

mechanical condition); very good (has minor cosmetic defects and is in excellent mechanical condition); good (has cosmetic defects that can be repaired and is free of major mechanical problems); and fair (has cosmetic defects and mechanical problems that require repair and/or replacement). In those evaluations, the book sets a range that varies depending on if you intend to trade in the car to a dealer or sell it to a private party. The advantage of the *Kelley Blue Book* is that it provides an objective and measurable quote for a used vehicle, regardless of where you live. Although I recommend using the *Kelley Blue Book* to establish legitimacy, I find that vehicle condition is a subjective standard that may undermine the Kelley Blue Book's integrity. The *Kelley Blue Book* site states that of the cars it values, 18 percent are in fair condition, 54 percent are in good condition, 23 percent are in very good condition, and 3 percent are in excellent condition. Although you may think your vehicle is in excellent or very good condition, it is highly likely the dealer will have a different perspective and that disparity will only complicate the negotiation.

2.   **NADA Guides***:* The official guide issued strictly for dealer members of the National Automobile Dealers Association trade group and lists wholesale and retail data based on exclusive data, including dealer retail sales, points-of-sale data, and other market data. The *NADA Guides* also provides valuations based on vehicle condition.

3.   **The Black Book**: The *Black Book* guide is restricted to dealers. It's issued every week and specializes in providing wholesale value in condition categories, including extra clean, clean, average, or rough. The *Black Book* also has values for rare or unusual vehicles in its "Cars of Particular Interest" listing.

4. **Trade-in price:** For a trade-in, the price is what another dealer or car-buying service will pay for the vehicle. Entities like CarMax will evaluate your vehicle and provide you with a purchase price. This process takes approximately an hour and is well worth the effort. If the dealer is unwilling to match that price, you have a very clear alternative.

5. **Used car desirability:** For a trade-in, the dealer may point to its ability to sell similarly equipped and conditioned cars on its lot or at an auction. It may also tell you what its used-car manager believes the car is worth on the day of the transaction.

6. **Advertisement:** For a new-car purchase, any advertisement from another dealer or website that reflects a more attractive offer—price or other terms—than what the dealer is currently offering. Don't let the dealer tell you that the offer doesn't apply to you, that you don't qualify, or that it is not credible. Buying a car from an out-of-state dealer is no more challenging than doing so from the dealer around the block. The dealer will be happy to take your call and facilitate all necessary logistics, including doing the paperwork and providing transportation. For the avoiders out there, you will never even need to meet the salesperson or set foot in the dealership.

7. **Dealer invoice:** Ask to see the dealer invoice for the vehicle. If the dealer won't let you see it, head for the exit—do not stop, do not look back.

8. **CARFAX report:** If you are buying a preowned car, ask to see its CARFAX report. It has the ownership history of the vehicle, the service records, the types of owners—business or personal—the locations of

ownership, the mileage, the ownership terms (purchase versus lease, business versus personal), the title history, and any accident or other damage. I would not purchase a preowned vehicle without carefully reviewing the CARFAX report and asking the dealer specific questions if the report show any accident or other damage involving the car. In particular, ask if the car has been repainted. If it has, ask why (accident or otherwise) the car was repainted. Even if the dealer says the car has not been repainted, check the gaps between the hood and trunk and the windshield as well as the gaps around the doors. Run your finger around the gap; it should feel nice and smooth. If it is at all rough, it is not a factory paint job. No matter what anyone says, there is only one time in the life of a vehicle when it has a factory paint job. Yes, you guessed it—when it leaves the factory.

9. **The car itself**: If you are trading in your vehicle, the car itself will serve as legitimacy for determining its value. How many miles are on the odometer? What is the condition of the paint? What about the interior? How does the engine run? This is not rocket science; the condition of a car generally speaks for itself.

10. **Window sticker:** The window sticker on a new car can also establish legitimacy in that it will tell you the vehicle's build/manufacture date. The longer the car has been sitting at the dealer, the more aggressive the dealer will be with pricing. When the salesperson tells you it is the hottest vehicle on the market and can't be discounted, the build date will provide legitimacy about the validity of that statement.

Car buying has evolved a lot, given the vast amounts of data available online. Both buyers and sellers can refer to a lot of data that will provide legitimacy and be an objective measuring stick. The parties can thus identify options that meet their interests and be the basis for any subsequent agreement and commitment. Although most legitimacy is objective, subjectivity is possible in the transaction. I strongly encourage you to use and maximize legitimacy to create a zone of potential agreement for the parties. If you discover that you aren't in this zone (an option better than your bottom line) or you believe that the options are unfair or not based in legitimacy, then take a deep breath, get up from your chair, and pursue your alternative.

CHAPTER

THIRTEEN

ALTERNATIVES—NO VELCRO ALLOWED

I am now ready to talk about alternatives or your best alternative to a negotiated agreement (BATNA). Remember that although options occur at the negotiating table, alternatives occur when you act unilaterally without the other party's agreement. Your BATNA is where you go when you walk away from the table; you can choose to go to your BATNA at any time during the negotiation.

I want to make sure you are crystal clear that your BATNA is strongest when you are buying a new car or trading in your old car. You should never feel entrapped when buying a new car. Just get up from the chair where you're sitting, grab the water and whatever may be left of your Otis Spunkmeyer cookies, and head calmly to the exit. This approach applies in all circumstances—whether you are buying a car in inventory, you have asked the dealer to find a car from another dealer, or you have special-ordered the vehicle (maybe you made a fully refundable deposit), and it has just arrived from the factory.

To recap, it is your ultimate objective to engage in an effective negotiation. In other words, you can successfully communicate with the party and maintain a good working relationship. Doing this should help you to uncover the interests of the parties; these interests lead to beneficial, legitimate options that create value for both parties. In many negotiations, this approach yields an option that meets the parties' interests, and an agreement can be reached. However, that is not always the case and you may have to realize that it may be better to walk away and go to your BATNA—the best alternative to negotiated agreement.

BATNA is based on the premise that any agreement with another party must be better than your alternative. That concept makes perfect sense in theory but is much more difficult to follow in practice. Going to BATNA, or even thinking about it, is very difficult for many parties and requires strong discipline. Despite that fear and anxiety, it is crucial that BEFORE you enter into a negotiation, you identify your BATNA and the BATNA of the other party. Once you know your BATNA, you may need to disclose it during the negotiation (in either a threatening or nonthreatening way) and reality-test the legitimacy of the other party's BATNA if the party does the same thing (optimally, in a peaceful mode). Your mission, should you choose to accept it, is to improve your BATNA during the negotiation and legitimately worsen the BATNA of the other party.

Always know your BATNA before the negotiation begins. Knowing this is absolutely important when you find yourself sitting in the chair at the car dealership negotiating the purchase price for your new car and the value of your trade-in. If you can't agree on the terms with the salesperson, you must go to your BATNA. And it is then that you must exercise absolute discipline.

Car dealerships are intelligent; they invite you in to see the new car you're interested in or the car you special-ordered. The dealer washes, waxes, and shines up the tires, and puts the car squarely in your sight line in the middle of the showroom, sometimes on a checkered floor under a disco light. The dealer lets you carefully inspect the car. You feel the factory paint job. You sit inside and grab the steering wheel, and take in that new-car smell. You begin to daydream about driving down the highway on a perfect summer day with the top down and radio blaring. News flash: You have just become entrapped.

Before I get into a specific BATNA analysis for your car-buying experience, let's discuss the general principles of BATNA. They are as follows:

1. **BATNA is not constant.** Alternatives change over time. Just because you have an iron-clad BATNA on Day 1 of the negotiation does not mean that it can't deteriorate by Day 20. The same applies to the other party; he may have a strong BATNA on Day 1 and may assert his BATNA early and often. Remember that BATNA strength may ebb and flow significantly during the negotiation.

2. **Personal and organizational BATNA may conflict.** Always know the difference between personal BATNA and organizational BATNA. In the car-buying context, is the BATNA of the dealership the same as that of the salesperson? Think about how a disparity between personal and organizational BATNA may affect the negotiation.

3. **BATNA is a dangerous weapon.** Be careful when you assert your BATNA, as the other party can perceive it as a threat. If you do throw it out there, be prepared for the other side to test its legitimacy.

4. **Once you pull the trigger, BATNA, like a bullet, is in motion.** If you are going to assert your BATNA and leave the table, then you must be ready to do so and accept 100 percent of the consequences.

5. **You are free to leave at any time.** Neither party should ever feel entrapped in the negotiation. Both parties have a decision to make and any agreement should be better than their alternative. If it is not, then walking away is a reasonable and prudent decision.

6. **At what point will you walk away?** It is important to distinguish between your bottom line (the least acceptable option that you will agree to) and pursuing your alternative. Remember that options are ideas that happen at the negotiating table, whereas alternatives are unilateral actions you can take away from the table without the other party's consent or participation.

7. **Preparation is critical.** Know your bottom line and BATNA <u>before</u> you start negotiating. Are you limited to a particular budget? Do you need to receive a certain amount for your trade-in to satisfy a loan balance on the vehicle? Again, you have to know the point at which you believe you have exhausted all possible options that will fulfill your interests and then head for the door.

8. **How strong is your BATNA?** Think carefully about how your BATNA strength versus that of the other party may affect your negotiation strategy. Think of these options:

   a. *Both parties have a strong BATNA*: If both parties have a strong BATNA, then the question becomes "so what now?" Since both parties have a viable place to walk to if they can't reach an agreement, this should help facilitate an effective negotiation based on honest, open, and candid communication. In the car-buying context, I buy the car elsewhere, and the dealership sells the car to another customer.

   b. *You have a strong BATNA and the other party has a weak BATNA*: What should you do? Be as aggressive as possible and take the other party to the cleaners? Gut the other party like a pig? I will leave these choices to your discretion. Think of how your actions may affect a long-term relationship. Do you really care about your relationship with the car dealer? Not really. You are going to get the best deal you can and not even think twice about how the dealership or salesperson might be affected—period.

c. *You have a weak BATNA and the other party has a strong BATNA*: The other party will be going through the same analysis in Scenario B above. What will you do? Cave in? Grovel? It is hard to imagine this scenario in the car-buying context unless you are buying a very limited-production vehicle and the dealership has the only car available in the country. If you are faced with this scenario, you still have a BATNA and should not feel entrapped. Put on your blinders and do not look at the car you have been coveting for six months that is sitting under the disco light.

d. *Both parties have a weak BATNA*: This is when you should exercise extreme caution. Again, this is hard to imagine in the car-buying context because another dealer or another customer is always available. If this scenario occurs, you are likely going to be playing a game of chicken and that never ends well.

If we think about going into the car dealership to buy a new car and possibly trade in our old car, you will generally find yourself in Scenario

B—you have a strong BATNA and the dealership has a weak BATNA. I have reached this conclusion by doing a BATNA analysis, as follows:

Car-Buyer BATNA:

1. Go to another dealer—in the same city, same state, or other state. The Internet has placed the world at your fingertips.

2. Leave and come back at another time, perhaps the end of the month when the dealer might have more of an incentive to meet your price or other terms.

3. Call another dealer while you are in the middle of the negotiation and tell the dealer about the situation. Ask the dealer if it will beat the deal you have on the table. If so, use that information to strengthen your BATNA.

4. In accordance with No. 3, leave and go to the other dealer.

5. Do nothing—wait for the dealership to react to your demands on price or other terms.

6. Defer the new-car purchase for a while.

7. Sell your car to a private party.

8. Sell your car to a car-buying service, such as CarMax.

9. Donate your car and take the charitable deduction.

10. Give your car to a friend or family member.

11. If you are dealing with the salesperson, escalate the negotiation and deal with the sales manager. If you are

dealing with the sales manager, escalate to the dealer general manager.

12. Buy a completely different vehicle—different manufacturer or model.

13. Rent a car for a while to confirm your choice.

14. Borrow a car from a friend or family member until you can secure terms that fulfill your interests

15. Walk, ride a bicycle, or use public transportation.

16. Buy a preowned car.

17. Buy a membership to Zipcar or other car-sharing service.

18. Hire the Rebel Negotiator to negotiate on your behalf.

Salesperson/Dealership BATNA:

1. Sell the car to another customer.

2. Do nothing—wait for the customer to react to your price and terms.

3. Sell or trade the car to another dealer.

Based upon this analysis, I would prefer to be on the side of the buyer. Always remember your BATNA when you enter the car dealership. Don't get entrapped. Don't get caught up in the new-car smell or the perfect factory paint job. And do not, in any circumstance, look at the disco light. Remember, you are not Velcroed in the chair. If the salesperson or dealership won't agree to an option that meets your interests, sit up, take a deep breath, tell them thanks for the time, and walk out the door.

CHAPTER  FOURTEEN

COMMITMENT—ARE YOU AUTHORIZED TO MAKE THAT DECISION?

A commitment is a statement or a binding promise that reflects a party's obligations. Good commitments are realistic, well planned, free from ambiguity, and can be implemented or executed against. There are three types of commitment in a negotiation. First, there is the parties' commitment to the process of the negotiation. Second, there is the commitment to an option that meets the parties' interests. Third, there is a commitment at the end of the negotiation to formalize the parties' commitment and to execute their obligations in the agreement.

When arriving at the dealership and meeting the salesperson, you must get a commitment to the process of the negotiation. If you are trading in a car, you will need to have the manager evaluate the preowned car and come up with a price. One of the most common complaints by new-car purchasers is how long it takes to complete the transaction. I encourage you to make it very clear to the salesperson that you have no intention of spending the entire day in the dealership. I would recommend telling the salesperson that you have a commitment in two hours and will walk way if you can't reach an agreement by then.

If he wants your business, he will expedite the trade-in evaluation as well as come up with the terms for the new car. If he is not operating in that time frame, then leave the dealership. You must make it clear that you say what you mean and you mean what you say. If you commit to two hours, then that is the timeline you'll work in. Remember, the dealer wants to keep you in that seat as long as possible, wear you out, make you look at the new car of your dreams, and make you feel entrapped. If you've carefully read this book, you will not fall for that tactic.

When you've agreed on a process, it is time to communicate interests and discuss options. I encourage you to be as direct as possible with the dealership about the new-car price and trade-in value. If the trade-in value is too low, then focus on legitimacy as the foundation for a higher price. Don't be afraid to say what you believe to be a market-relevant price, given the condition and mileage of the vehicle. Do the same with a new car. Ask to see the invoice and offer a purchase price based upon the breadth of legitimacy you have assembled. If you can find an option that meets your interests, you can move forward to the next stage of commitment. If you can't find an acceptable option, then head for the door to determine the appropriate next steps. Whatever you do, do not split oranges and do not be afraid to assert and execute your BATNA.

One key component of the second commitment is the authority of the parties conducting the negotiation. Although there could be exceptions, I will assume that you are fully empowered and authorized to reach an agreement with the dealership. You can make a commitment and move forward with the purchase. As you know, the discussion about options, the price of the new car, and the value of the trade-in have multiple steps. In each step, the salesperson will get up from his desk and walk down the hall to discuss your offer with the sales manager. Ultimately, the sales manager is empowered to commit the dealership.

The Rebel Negotiator encourages you to bypass the salesperson and negotiate directly with the sales manager. Why waste time negotiating with someone who lacks the power to commit to price or terms? If the sales manager refuses to negotiate with you, then leave the dealership and go elsewhere.

Remember that you have an extremely strong BATNA. You don't need to do anything. If the sales manager refuses to negotiate with you, you don't like the attitude of the salesperson, or you don't like the color of the carpet, just leave. I can't stress this point enough. Do not split oranges, do not compromise, do not accept an option that doesn't fulfill your interests, and do not get entrapped. Know your BATNA, assert your BATNA, and exercise your BATNA freely. Even if you're afraid, visit a local car dealership and practice this technique. Pretend that you are interested in buying a new car. Talk with a salesperson or the sales manager. Offer a price. When it is not accepted, walk diligently toward the door. If it is accepted, then keep asking for more until they say no and then walk to the door.

The final stage of commitment will come after you have agreed to BOTH a trade-in price and new-car purchase price that meet your interests. If either component of the transaction does not meet your interests, then go to your BATNA. Once you have agreed on terms, you will then be ushered into the finance office to complete myriad paperwork. Even though you are in the finance office, you can still walk away from the transaction—even if hands have been shaken, and the temporary tags are being affixed. If you don't like the financing terms, go to your BATNA. Don't be entrapped. You can always come back tomorrow, and I guarantee they will be waiting for you with open arms.

The final word is: Don't be in a rush to make a commitment. Slow down, listen for interests, and think about options. Once there is an option that meets your interests, you can agree and make a commitment. Don't get entrapped and don't split the difference in any circumstance.

CHAPTER

FIFTEEN

A BLUE-RIBBON RECIPE

I want to make it clear that the negotiation framework I have previously described applies to all buyers, regardless of gender. According to research from Carnegie Mellon University, women do not assume as many things are negotiable and miss opportunities to negotiate. They see negotiation as conflict and avoid negotiations completely, struggle in ambiguous situations, and are judged more harshly when they negotiate or advocate on their behalf.

One of the primary reasons why women miss opportunities to negotiate is ascribed to the "asking advantage." This advantage suggests that women worry more than men about the effect their actions will have on their relationships. Ultimately, this results in a desire to protect personal connections, which manifests itself in asking for things indirectly or asking for less.

When I am asked how we can best address the gender differences in negotiation, I point to my recipe for being a successful negotiator because it is gender agnostic. If you're concerned about the relationship, the beauty of the new-car purchase is that the relationship with the car salesperson and dealership is purely transactional and, as we have discussed, 100 percent of the focus should be on the issues. If we are friends after the ink has dried, great. If not, no tears will be shed.

A female buyer should not feel anxious, nervous, or stressed upon entering the car dealership. Women should channel their inner Rebel Negotiator: Be assertive and don't worry about the relationship. Say what you mean and mean what you say. Prepare diligently, focus on interests, consider all options, and maximize legitimacy. And most important, remember the strength of your BATNA.

CHAPTER

SIXTEEN

RULES OF THE ROAD

Now that you have read this book, you should be ready to buy your new car. I will leave you with a list of my key principles and rules of the road that you can quickly refer to when you are in the middle of your negotiation:

1. Never let your relationship with the car salesperson affect your buying decision.

2. You can always use negative-influence techniques, such as manipulation (lies and deceit), intimidation (loud and abrasive verbal aggressiveness), avoidance (doing nothing), or threats (comply with my desire, or else).

3. Don't play games like these: bidding against yourself, positional bargaining that results in compromise, caving in because you feel heavily invested in the process, playing chicken, rewarding anchoring, or making decisions based upon your perceived level of entrapment.

4. You will never have a stronger BATNA than when you enter a car dealership to trade in the old car and

purchase a new one—period. There are no exceptions to this rule. I don't care if you like the dealership, like the salesperson, love the car, like the free Otis Spunkmeyer cookies, or whatever your excuse; you are not and will never be entrapped when buying a new car.

5. If you don't know your goal, then you might as well call it a day and play golf.

6. Regarding preparation, remember what Coach Coughlin said: humble enough to prepare, confident enough to perform.

7. Know that the actual negotiation may not flow as smoothly as it did when you role-played in front of the mirror or with your friends, family, or office colleagues.

8. Temper your approach based upon the amount of risk in delivery. (Will you consider a preowned car? A dealer demo model? A different color, model, or set of options than originally contemplated?)

9. Temper your approach based on where you live. (How you approach the salesperson in New York may be different from how you approach the salesperson in Omaha.)

10. Temper your approach based upon the people sitting across from you at the negotiation table. (In a car dealership, this is likely to be the salesperson as well as the sales manager.)

11. Remember that conflicts are created, conducted, and sustained by human beings, and can be resolved by human beings. (It's just a new car—there's no need to get overly stressed or anxious.)

12. Remember the words of Harvey Specter from the television show *Suits*: "What are your choices when someone puts a gun to your head? What are you talking about? You do what they say or they shoot you. WRONG. You take the gun, or you pull out a bigger one. Or, you call their bluff. Or, you do one of a hundred and forty-six other things."

13. As I previously discussed, preparation is an absolute necessity for any negotiation and even more so for delivering a difficult message. I can't stress enough the importance of thorough preparation. Make sure that you have an in-depth understanding of the issues and that you focus on legitimacy.

14. Seek to understand instead of seeking to be understood. The difference may seem subtle, but it is significant and will absolutely affect the tone and tenor of your conversation. Use inquiry instead of advocacy, and find the right balance between diplomacy and directness.

15. Prepare yourself for a negative reaction. The conversation may become tense. Your preparation should help you be emotionally ready. Keep your competitive arousal in check—ask yourself, do you want to be right or be effective?

16. Keep things in perspective. How significant are the message and the issue? Will it even matter in six months? In six years?

17. Be a good LIAR—listen, inquire, acknowledge and respond.

18. Once you think you have exhausted the list of potential options, think again. Be open to considering

all options; rather than saying no, think about under what conditions you might say yes.

19. Once you walk into the dealership, you must follow this rule: You are not here to build relationships with anyone and will not let any relationship, real, perceived, or otherwise, influence your decision-making process—period.

20. How often do you buy a new car? Do you think it will matter in two, four, or five years, what, if any, relationship you built with the salesperson?

21. What is the probability that the salesperson will even be around for the next purchase? The 2015 National Automobile Dealers Association annual *Dealership Workforce Study* reported that sales consultant turnover is 71.9 percent annually.

22. Even if you build a relationship, what level of authority does the salesperson even have to dictate the purchase price and terms?

23. Other than nominal concessions on a detail or an extra set of floor mats, what special treatment or incentives have you received based upon having an excellent and sustained relationship with your salesperson?

24. Given the level of competitiveness in the industry, do you really think the dealership will turn you away if you don't seek BFF status with its sales personnel?

25. What do you think the relationship will get you? Will it yield a candid, honest, and straightforward conversation? Do you really think you are going to get better prices or better terms?

26. If you still want to build a relationship, you can, but remember to separate the relationship from the substance of the negotiation.

27. In no circumstance should you ever agree to split oranges.

28. Ask to see the dealer invoice for the specific vehicle you intend to buy. If the dealer won't let you see the invoice, head for the exit—do not stop and do not look back.

29. Your BATNA strength in buying a new car or trading in your old car is at its strongest. Under no circumstance should you ever feel entrapped.

30. It is crucial that BEFORE you enter into negotiation that you identify your BATNA and the BATNA of the other party.

31. Know your BATNA before you start negotiating.

32. If you are going to assert your BATNA and leave the table, then you must be ready to do so and accept 100 percent of the consequences.

33. It is important to distinguish between your bottom line (the least acceptable option that you will agree to) and pursuing your alternative. Remember that options are ideas that happen at the negotiating table, whereas alternatives are unilateral actions you can take away from the table without the other party's consent or participation.

34. Don't get caught up in the new-car smell or the perfect factory paint job. And don't in any circumstance look at the disco light. Remember, you are not Velcroed in

the chair. If the salesperson or dealership won't agree to an option that meets your interests, sit up, take a deep breath, tell them thanks for their time, and walk out the door.

35. Commit to a process before the negotiation begins.

36. If the sales manager refuses to negotiate with you, you don't like the attitude of the salesperson, or you don't like the color of the carpet, just leave.

37. Do not split oranges, do not compromise, do not accept an option that doesn't fulfill your interests, and do not get entrapped.

38. Slow down, listen for interests, and think about options.

39. Female buyers should not feel anxious, nervous, or stressed upon entering the car dealership. Channel your inner Rebel Negotiator: Be assertive and don't worry about the relationship. Prepare diligently, focus on interests, consider all options, and maximize legitimacy.

40. Remember, the dealer wants to keep you in that seat as long as possible, wear you out, make you look at the new car of your dreams, and make you feel entrapped. Because you have carefully read this book, you will not fall for these tactics.

Now that you have these key rules and principles, I hope to see you navigating down the street in your new car.

ABOUT — THE — AUTHOR

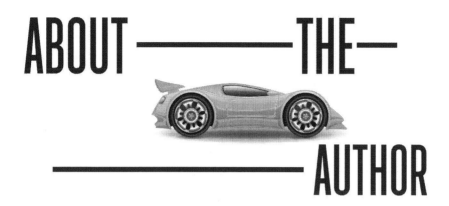

Grant S. Lange, the Rebel Negotiator, is a partner and member of the Negotiations Center of Excellence for a leading IT services company and has served in a variety of leadership roles at some of the world's largest IT services, advisory, and software firms. During the day, he is responsible for negotiating large, complex, and strategic consulting, technology, and outsourcing agreements; building trusted adviser relationships with legal, finance, and procurement executives across the Fortune 500 client community; developing thought leadership on the art and science of negotiation; and training his colleagues how to fine-tune their negotiation skills. During his career, the Rebel Negotiator has successfully negotiated services agreements that have generated more than $5 billion in new sales.

During his spare time, the Rebel Negotiator rides motorcycles, lifts weights, drives fast cars, and shoots guns. And he will always find time to help a colleague, friend, family member, or reader negotiate the purchase of a new car.

Made in the USA
San Bernardino, CA
29 November 2019